Desert Animals

Jackrabbits

by Emily Rose Townsend

Consulting Editor: Gail Saunders-Smith, Ph.D.

Consultant: Michael A. Mares, Ph.D.
Director, Sam Noble Oklahoma Museum
of Natural History, University of Oklahoma
Norman, Oklahoma

Pobbie Books

Pebble Books are published by Capstone Press
151 Good Counsel Drive, P.O. Box 669, Mankato, Minnesota 56002
http://www.capstone-press.com

1 2 3 4 5 6 08 07 06 05 04 03

Library of Congress Cataloging-in-Publication Data
Townsend, Emily Rose.
   Jackrabbits / by Emily Rose Townsend.
   p. cm.—(Desert animals)
   Includes bibliographical references (p. 23) and index.
   ISBN 0-7368-2076-0 (hardcover)
   1. Jackrabbits—Juvenile literature. [1. Jackrabbits. 2. Hares.] I. Title.
QL737.L32 T68 2004
599.32′2—dc21
                                                                2002154581

Summary: Simple text and photographs describe jackrabbits that live in deserts.

Note to Parents and Teachers

The Desert Animals series supports national science standards related to life science. This book describes and illustrates jackrabbits that live in deserts. The photographs support early readers in understanding the text. The repetition of words and phrases helps early readers learn new words. This book also introduces early readers to subject-specific vocabulary words, which are defined in the Glossary section. Early readers may need assistance to read some words and to use the Table of Contents, Glossary, Read More, Internet Sites, and Index/Word List sections of the book.

Table of Contents

Jackrabbits

Jackrabbits are mammals with big ears. Jackrabbits are hares. Hares are bigger than rabbits.

Most jackrabbits
live alone.

deserts where jackrabbits live

Deserts

Many jackrabbits live
in deserts in the
United States and Mexico.

Body Parts

Jackrabbits have tan, gray, black, or white fur.

Jackrabbits have long ears. Their ears help keep them cool by getting rid of heat.

Jackrabbits have strong hind legs and feet. Jackrabbits hop and leap.

What Jackrabbits Do

Jackrabbits run fast
to escape predators.
Coyotes, cougars, eagles,
and hawks eat jackrabbits.

18

Jackrabbits eat plants, shrubs, grass, and twigs.

Jackrabbits rest in the shade most of the day. They hop around the desert at night.

Glossary

coyote—an animal similar to a wolf

desert—an area that is very dry; very little rain falls in deserts.

escape—to avoid or get away from

hare—an animal similar to a rabbit; hares have longer ears and longer hind legs than rabbits; unlike rabbits, hares are born covered with fur and with their eyes open.

hawk—a bird that eats many small animals; hawks usually have rounded wings and a long tail.

hind leg—the back leg of an animal; jackrabbits have strong hind legs.

mammal—a warm-blooded animal that has a backbone; mammals have hair or fur.

Mexico—a country in southern North America

predator—an animal that hunts other animals for food

shrub—a short bush

Read More

Auch, Alison. *Desert Animals*. Spyglass Books. Minneapolis: Compass Point Books, 2003.

Butterfield, Moira. *Animals in Hot Places*. Looking At. Austin, Texas: Raintree Steck-Vaughn, 2000.

Galko, Francine. *Desert Animals*. Animals in Their Habitats. Chicago: Heinemann Library, 2003.

Internet Sites

Do you want to find out more about jackrabbits? Let FactHound, our fact-finding hound dog, do the research for you.

Here's how:

1) Visit *http://www.facthound.com*

2) Type in the **Book ID** number: **0736820760**

3) Click on **FETCH IT**.

FactHound will fetch Internet sites picked by our editors just for you!

Index/Word List

cool, 13
day, 21
desert, 9, 21
ears, 5, 13
eat, 17, 19
escape, 17
feet, 15
fur, 11
grass, 19

hares, 5
heat, 13
hop, 15, 21
leap, 15
legs, 15
live, 7, 9
mammals, 5
Mexico, 9
night, 21

plants, 19
predators, 17
rest, 21
run, 17
shade, 21
shrubs, 19
twigs, 19
United States, 9

Word Count: 99
Early-Intervention Level: 13

Editorial Credits
Mari C. Schuh, editor; Patrick D. Dentinger, designer; Kelly Garvin, photo researcher;
   Karen Risch, product planning editor

Photo Credits
Bill Everitt/Tom Stack & Associates, 1, 6
Bruce Coleman, Inc./Jeff Foott, cover; Larry R. Ditto, 4, 18; Robert Carr, 12;
   Lee Rentz, 14; Michael Fogden, 16
Comstock Klips, 8
Gerald & Buff Corsi/Visuals Unlimited, 10
Tom Stack/Tom Stack & Associates, 20